This
Book
Belongs
To _____

*Dedicated to the memory of P. J. Becker.
He fought valiantly his entire life and had the heart
of a champion. We will miss you, but never forget your
zest for life. May God be with you and your family.*

GEORGE AND ROBERT

The scripture quotations contained herein are from the New Revised Standard Version Bible: Catholic Edition ©1989 by the Division of Christian Education of the National Council of the Churches of Christ in the U.S.A. Used by permission. All rights reserved.

This edition published by permission of Thomas Nelson, Inc.

Text copyright © by C. R. Gibson®

C.R. Gibson is a registered trademark of Thomas Nelson, Inc.

Published by Regina Press

Printed in Belgium

All rights reserved

ISBN 088271 527 5

An **ALICE IN BIBLELAND** Storybook

CATHOLIC EDITION

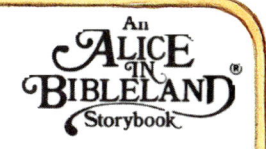

The GOOD SHEPHERD

Written by Alice Joyce Davidson
Illustrated by Victoria Marshall

Regina Press New York

A little girl named Alice
Went to visit friends one day.

They lived out in the country
And had lots of room to play.

They packed a little picnic lunch,
A favorite book or two,

Then climbed up on a grassy hill
Where they had quite a view.

Alice watched some sheep graze
As she sat beneath a tree,

Then she took her Bible out
And read Psalm Twenty-three.

As a youth, King David
Was a shepherd all day long.

And while he watched his father's sheep,
He wrote this special song.

Alice loved Psalm Twenty-three
And the promise that it brought.

She wrote some special poems
To help explain each thought.

She read them to her friends that day
And then when she was through

She wrote them on this little pad
To share them now with you.

The Lord is my shepherd…

The Lord is my Shepherd,
I'm glad this is so,
For I'm one of His sheep
And He helps me to grow.

The Lord is my Shepherd,
How joyous to know

He's always beside me
Wherever I go!

I shall not want...

The air I breathe, the food I eat,
The flowers blooming by my feet,
The Lord gives these to me.
My family and friends to love,
The sun that shines down from above,
The Lord gives these to me.

A little work, some games to play,
Pets to care for every day,
The Lord gives these to me.

New things to learn, and books to read,
Everything I ever need,
The Lord gives these to me.

*He makes me lie down
in green pastures…*

A shepherd knows
His little sheep
Need time to run
And time to sleep.

The Lord, too, knows
That everyone
Needs safe sound sleep
When day is done.

The Lord will watch us
Through the night
And keep us safe
'Til morning's light.

*He leads me beside
still waters...*

Just as a shepherd leads his flock
To waters that are still,
And makes sure that his sheep are safe
Until they drink their fill...

Our Lord and Shepherd leads us
In His kind and gentle way

Away from harm and danger
To a good life every day.

He restores my soul...

Little sheep are happy.
They romp and play and bleat;
But if they stumble, they need help
To get back on their feet.

The same is true of all of us.
We stumble now and then,

And, God, our Shepherd, reaches out
And lifts us up again.

*He leads me
in right paths
for his name's sake...*

Sheep have funny habits.
They all just tag along.
And go with one another
Even if the way is wrong.

But we're not sheep and so we know
That should we go astray,

God will lead us back again
In His gentle, loving way.

*Even though I walk
through the darkest valley,*

*I fear no evil;
for you are with me...*

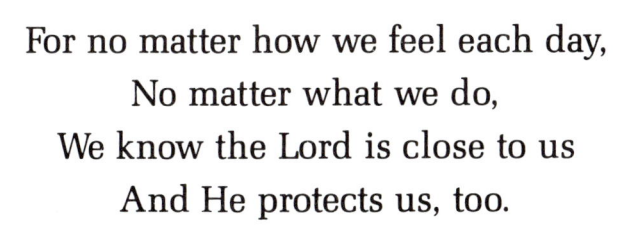

For no matter how we feel each day,
No matter what we do,
We know the Lord is close to us
And He protects us, too.

Sometimes when we are sick in bed
Our hearts are filled with gloom,
But there is nothing we should fear—
The Lord is in our room...

*Your rod and staff –
they comfort me...*

The shepherd has two special tools
He carries in each arm:
A sturdy staff and trusty rod
Protect his flock from harm.

The Lord, our Shepherd, keeps us, too,
From anything that harms.

He cares for us and comforts us
Within His loving arms.

*You prepare a table before me
in the presence of my enemies...*

No matter what we need in life,
However big or small,
The Lord, our Shepherd, knows our needs
And He provides them all.

And when we feel there's danger
Anywhere around us,

We know our Lord is with us—
His loving care surrounds us!

*You anoint my head
with oil; my cup
overflows...*

God gives to me,
God gives to you
The sun, the stars,
The sky of blue...

Birds that sing,
Springtime showers,
Butterflies,
And fragrant flowers.

Loving families,
Special friends—
Our list of blessings
Never ends!

*Surely goodness and mercy
shall follow me all
the days
of my life...*

I may be very young yet,
But still in all I know
The Lord will guide and bless me
And be with me as I grow.

And years and years and years from now,
When I'm a grownup, too,

I know the Lord will be with me
Each day my whole life through!

*And I shall dwell in
the house of the Lord
my whole life long.*

Dear Lord, I love you very much
And hope that I can be
As good to everyone I know
As you are good to me.

Dear Lord, I love you very much
And hope that I can stay

Dear to You and near to You
Forever and a day!

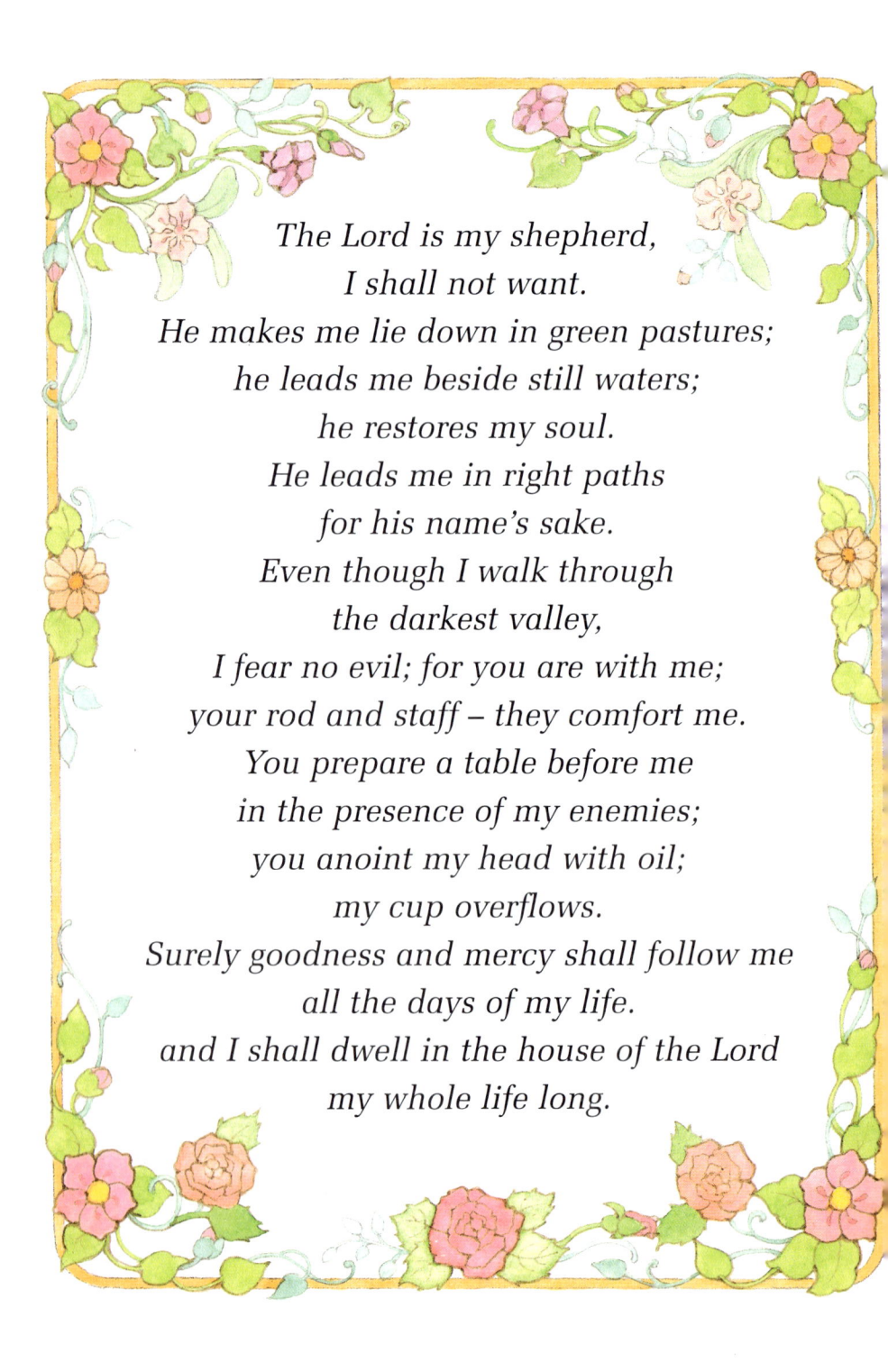

*The Lord is my shepherd,
I shall not want.
He makes me lie down in green pastures;
he leads me beside still waters;
he restores my soul.
He leads me in right paths
for his name's sake.
Even though I walk through
the darkest valley,
I fear no evil; for you are with me;
your rod and staff – they comfort me.
You prepare a table before me
in the presence of my enemies;
you anoint my head with oil;
my cup overflows.
Surely goodness and mercy shall follow me
all the days of my life.
and I shall dwell in the house of the Lord
my whole life long.*

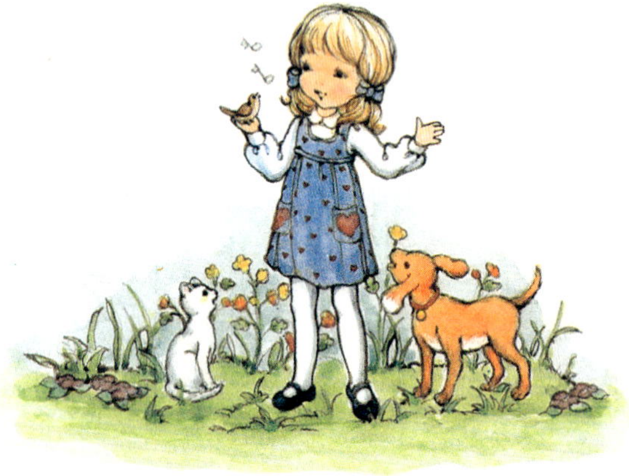